'If you like *The Kite Runner*, you'll love *The Little Coffee Shop of Kabul*. This compelling story of a cafe in the heart of Afghanistan, and the men and women who meet there, is full of heart and intelligence'

Look magazine on *The Little Coffee Shop of Kabul*

'An eye-opening and uplifting tale about sisterhood and survival'

Grazia on *The Little Coffee Shop of Kabul*

'A brilliant story of strength and appreciation of difference that restores belief in humanity'

Daily Telegraph on *The Little Coffee Shop of Kabul*

'A novel of female friendship and support when East meets West, of magic and things we may not understand, of hope, of comfort, and in the background the enticing salty, fishy, spicy aromas of Zanzibar'

Dinah Jeffries on *The Zanzibar Wife*

'A compelling account of three very different women, each challenged by circumstances that reveal the inner conflict in their lives, and their refusal to conform. The book is also a glowing portrait of Oman, a country that for many in the west remains an enigma. The author uses her canvas to bring this unique culture to life, whilst crafting a deft and emotionally engaging tale'

Vaseem Khan on *The Zanzibar Wife*

Also by Deborah Rodriguez

FICTION

The Little Coffee Shop of Kabul

Return to the Little Coffee Shop of Kabul

The Zanzibar Wife

Island on the Edge of the World

NON-FICTION

The Kabul Beauty School

The House on Carnaval Street

The
Moroccan
Daughter

DEBORAH
RODRIGUEZ

sphere

SPHERE

First published in Australia in 2021 by Bantam,
a division of Penguin Random House Australia
First published in Great Britain in 2021 by Sphere

13 5 7 9 10 8 6 4 2

A CIP catalogue record for this book is available from the British Library.

ISBN 978-0-7515-7460-9

Printed and bound in Great Britain by Clays Ltd, Elcograf S.p.A.

Papers used by Sphere are from well-managed forests
and other responsible sources.

Sphere
An imprint of
Little, Brown Book Group
Carmelite House
50 Victoria Embankment
London EC4Y 0DZ

An Hachette UK Company
www.hachette.co.uk

www.littlebrown.co.uk

To all my beautiful friends.
My life is richer because of you.

Be with those who help your being.

RUMI